THE
TEXAS WAR
OF INDEPENDENCE
THE 1800s

BY
RICHARD WORTH

 **Marshall Cavendish**
Benchmark
New York

Thanks to Stephen Pitti, professor of history and American studies at Yale University,
for his expert reading of this manuscript.

MARSHALL CAVENDISH BENCHMARK
99 WHITE PLAINS ROAD
TARRYTOWN, NEW YORK 10591-5502
www.marshallcavendish.us

LIBRARY OF CONGRESS CATALOGING-IN-PUBLICATION DATA
Worth, Richard.
The Texas war of independence / by Richard Worth.
p. cm. — (Hispanic America)
Summary: "Provides comprehensive information on the history of Spanish exploration in the United States,
focusing on the Texas Revolt and the Mexican War"—Provided by publisher. Includes index.
ISBN 978-0-7614-2934-0
1. Texas—History—To 1846—Juvenile literature.
2. Texas—History—Revolution, 1835-1836—Juvenile literature.
3. Southwest, New—History—To 1848—Juvenile literature.
4. Mexican War, 1846-1848—Juvenile literature.
5. Mexican Americans—Texas—Social conditions—19th century—Juvenile literature.
6. Mexican Americans—Southwest, New—Social conditions—19th century—Juvenile literature. I. Title.
F390.W93 2009
976.4'04—dc22
2007029478

Photo research by Linda Sykes

Front and Back cover photo: The Granger Collection
The photographs in this book are used by permission and through the courtesy of:
The Granger Collection: 1, 15, 16, 22, 23, 34, 36, 41, 42-43, 53, 56-57, 60, 63, 66, 72. Alamy: The Print
Collector, 4; Interfoto Pressebildagentur 9; North Wind Picture Archives, 18. Corbis: Bettmann, 12, 33;
PoodlesRock, 24. Library of Congress: 27. Texas State Capitol Art Collection, Texas State Preservation Board:
29, 37, 46. The San Jacinto Museum of History, Houston: 39. www.galleryoftherepublic.com: 50. Art Resource,
NY: National Portrait Gallery, Smithsonian Institution, Washington D. C.: 62. de Saisset Museum, Santa Clara
University: Museum permanent collection, Gift of Monserrat Roca 1.756, 69. Bancroft Library, University of
California, Berkeley: 71.

EDITOR: Joy Bean   PUBLISHER: Michelle Bisson
ART DIRECTOR: Anahid Hamparian   SERIES DESIGNER: Kristen Branch

Printed in China
1 3 5 6 4 2

CONTENTS

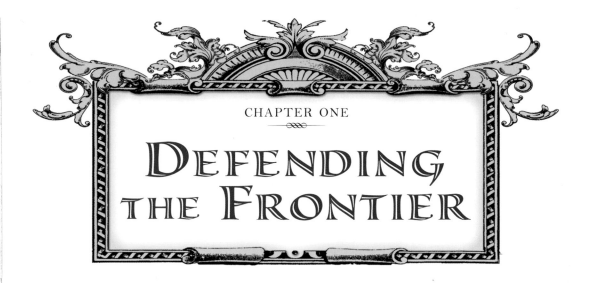

CHAPTER ONE

DEFENDING THE FRONTIER

I N 1806, LIEUTENANT FACUNDO MELGARES gathered an expedition of more than five hundred soldiers on the town plaza of Santa Fe, the capital of Spanish New Mexico. Since 1492, when Christopher Columbus first sailed to America, the Spanish had conquered a vast empire in the New World. Spain's new territory included much of the Caribbean, South America, Mexico, the North American Southwest, and California. At first, the Spanish had come to the New World searching for gold and silver. Then they built Catholic churches to convert the Native Americans, constructed forts to defend their empire, and established towns like Santa Fe.

A stocky, dark-haired man, Melgares was a veteran of the Spanish army that defended the frontier. Perhaps this was

Opposite:
Spanish explorers began coming to the New World in search of wealth after Christopher Columbus arrived there in 1492.

the reason he had been chosen for this important mission by Commandant General Nemesio Salcedo. Commandant General Salcedo was in charge of the interior provinces. Established several decades earlier, the provinces included New Mexico, Arizona, and Texas. They had been combined under one command in order to help Spain defend its vast empire. Governed from Mexico City, Mexico, Spain's broad empire stretched from California eastward to the Texas border with Louisiana.

Lieutenant Melgares's mission was to find and stop an American expedition. Led by Meriwether Lewis and William Clark, the expedition was traveling along the Missouri River and heading westward. Lewis and Clark had been directed by President Thomas Jefferson to explore the land of the Louisiana Purchase. A vast expanse of wilderness, Louisiana had been purchased from France in 1803. Stretching for 800,000 square miles (2,071,990 square kilometers), it almost doubled the size of the United States and included the territory from the Mississippi River to the Rocky Mountains.

Commandant General Salcedo feared that the North Americans now posed a tremendous threat to Spain's empire. The Louisiana Purchase placed the North Americans right on the borders of the Spanish frontier. In fact, *Anglo* merchants had already begun appearing in Santa Fe. In addition, the United States was claiming that Texas was part of the Louisiana Purchase, and an Anglo army unit had taken over the small Spanish *presidio* at Los Adaes in east Texas.

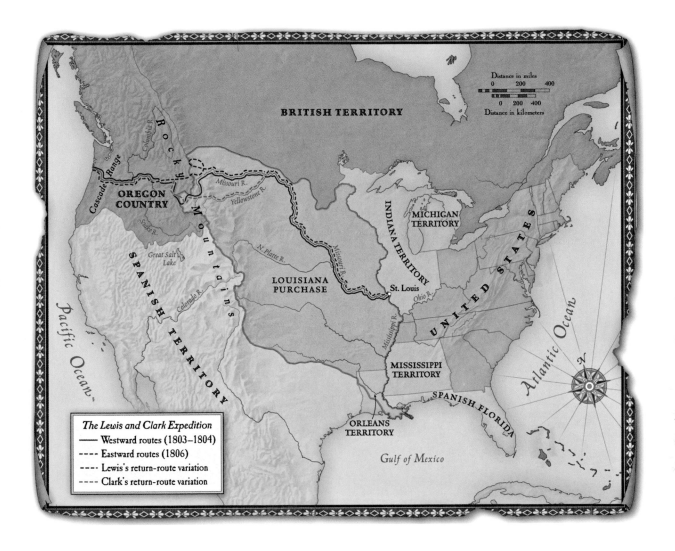

The Lewis and Clark Expedition
— Westward routes (1803–1804)
---- Eastward routes (1806)
---- Lewis's return-route variation
---- Clark's return-route variation

Almost 300,000 Anglo settlers already lived west of the Appalachian Mountains. Salcedo feared they might easily begin to move farther westward, eventually streaming into the Spanish colonies. Since the seventeenth century, these colonies had been only sparsely populated, with a mere three thousand settlers in Texas. Even fewer people lived in

California, and Tucson, the largest town in Arizona, had only one thousand inhabitants.

Commandant General Salcedo was also afraid that the Lewis and Clark expedition might disrupt Spanish relations with the western Native-American tribes. These relationships had reached a low point almost a century and a half earlier when Spanish *missionaries* had accompanied the settlers into New Mexico and Arizona. They had come to convert the local tribes to Christianity. Instead, the missionaries angered the Native Americans by criticizing their religious beliefs. Led by one of their religious leaders, or medicine men, the Pueblo Indians rose up in 1680. They killed hundreds of settlers and drove the Spanish out of New Mexico and Arizona. Eventually, Spain reconquered the area, but the Spanish were careful this time not to try to change the Native American's religious beliefs.

Meanwhile, Spain had to deal with other Native-American tribes as well, such as the Apache and Comanche. These dashing horsemen of the plains swooped down on Spanish settlements. They led cattle and sheep away from some Spanish *ranchos*, while killing settlers and missionaries. Albuquerque, located south of Santa Fe, was struck repeatedly by Native-American raiders. During the eighteenth century, Spain had tried to establish missions in east Texas, but the missionaries were driven out by Native-American raiding parties. Finally, in 1779, the Spanish managed to defeat the Comanche and kill their leader, Chief Cuerno Verde.

Seven years later, Pedro Vial—a Spanish trader respected by the tribes—helped bring peace to the frontier. He reminded the Comanche that they needed the Spanish traders because of the goods they brought. Without these traders, he said, "You do not have a knife to cut meat, a pot with which to cook, nor a grain of powder [or a musket] with which to kill deer and buffalo for your sustenance [food]," as historian John Kessell wrote in *Spain in the Southwest*. Soon afterward, the Comanche joined with the

Fed up with Spanish settlers who were trying to convert them to Christianity, Native Americans in the Southwest attacked the pioneers looking to settle in the late 1600s.

Spanish and helped them defeat the Apache. As a result, the Spanish frontier became far more peaceful, and settlers felt much safer.

But with the coming of the Lewis and Clark expedition, Spain feared that its now peaceful relationship with the Native Americans would be destroyed. The Spanish believed that U.S. merchants trading their goods with the various tribes might lessen the Native American's need to trade with the Spanish and therefore destroy Spain's alliance with the Native Americans. Spain worried that Spanish settlements might suddenly be in grave danger.

When Lieutenant Melgares set out with his soldiers in 1806, they were expected to locate and stop Lewis and Clark. In his search for the expedition, Melgares went only as far as present-day Nebraska. Over 100 miles (160.9 km) farther eastward, Lewis and Clark were already returning from their journey. Melgares traveled back to Santa Fe without ever locating the Anglo explorers, and by then it was too late to stop them.

In the early nineteenth century, Santa Fe was the biggest town in the Southwest, with a population of more than five thousand people. This included wealthy ranch owners, merchants, and small farmers. Life along the frontier could be harsh, and settlers regularly faced the possibility of death from hostile Native Americans. A man might be killed protecting his family, and his wife and children would be left to fend for themselves. As a result, women in Santa Fe often found themselves responsible for farms or stores that had once been owned by their husbands.

Upon his return to Santa Fe, Lieutenant Melgares met another Anglo traveler. In fall 1806, Lieutenant Zebulon Pike had been leading an expedition to explore the West. Caught in the heavy snows of winter, Pike and his men were eventually captured by the Spanish. They entered present-day southern Colorado, which had already been claimed by Spain as part of their vast empire. Pike was then taken to Santa Fe, where he met the Spanish governor, Joaquín Real Alencaster.

Word of Pike's capture reached Commandant General Salcedo. He ordered Melgares to escort Pike and his men out of the Spanish Empire and back to Louisiana. Along the way, twenty-seven-year-old Pike and Melgares became friendly. They stopped at Spanish settlements, where Pike was entertained at gala parties and met other Spanish military officers. They also visited Salcedo at his headquarters in Chihuahua, Mexico. Eventually though, Pike reached east Texas and crossed into Louisiana.

THE ANGLO THREAT

Although Lieutenant Pike had been removed from the Spanish Empire, the threat from the United States did not end for Spain. In 1806, war had almost broken out between the United States and Spain along the Texas border with

Lieutenant Zebulon Pike began exploring the West in 1806.

Louisiana. Eventually both nations agreed to establish the Neutral Ground. This strip of land, 30 miles (48.3 km) wide, was set up as a no-man's land between the two countries. But Spain was still worried that President Jefferson might try to press his demands that Texas should be part of the Louisiana Purchase. So in 1808, Texas governor Antonio Cordero sent out an expedition to make sure that no Anglo settlers had entered that region. Led by Francisco Amangual, an officer in his late sixties, the soldiers made a round trip between Santa Fe and Texas. But they found no Anglos.

SOLDIERS ON THE FRONTIER

The life of a soldier along the Spanish frontier was often lonely and dangerous. Soldiers lived in small presidios, or forts. Sometimes they were accompanied by their wives and families. But many soldiers had no families. The frontier was hundreds of miles from the Spanish capital in Mexico City. Soldiers reluctantly left this magnificent city, with its beautiful cathedrals and stately homes for dusty settlements like Santa Fe. Forgotten by people in the capital, they were expected to defend the frontier against Native-American attacks and Anglo invasions.

For those soldiers sent out to California or Texas, however, there might also be unusual opportunities not available in Mexico City. After serving for eighteen years, soldiers in California were awarded grants of land when they retired. José Maria Verdugo, for example, received a rancho of 166 square miles (430 square km). Luis Peralta, a retired sergeant in the army, received a land grant that included the area where the city of Oakland, California is now located. Some soldiers who performed their duties bravely could also look forward to advancement. Lieutenant Melgares, for example, eventually became governor of New Mexico.

A REVOLUTION IN MEXICO

While Spain's soldiers were busy guarding the empire, they were suddenly faced with a new threat. In 1808, the Spanish king Ferdinand VII was overthrown by the French. Emperor Napoleon Bonaparte led his armies into the Spanish capital, Madrid. Then he put his brother, Joseph, on the throne of Spain. These events sparked a revolution in Mexico. For many years, people called *criollos* had been displeased with the colonial government. The criollos had been barred from holding high political offices. Such important positions were reserved for *gachupines*. Many criollos felt no loyalty to the new French government, nor did they want to support Ferdinand VII, who had been driven off the throne. Many others in Mexico still supported Ferdinand because they regarded him as their King. So, in 1810, the criollos started a revolution to overthrow the Spanish government in Mexico.

Led by a criollo priest, Miguel Hidalgo, a huge army marched on Mexico City. Arriving at the gates of the capital,

Napoleon Bonaparte's brother, Joseph Bonaparte, became king of Spain in 1808 after being King of Naples and Sicily in Italy.

however, Hidalgo feared that his army was not strong enough to capture the city. Hidalgo fled, and his army was eventually defeated by Spanish armies loyal to Ferdinand VII. Hidalgo and a few followers headed north toward Texas. Here they hoped to give the revolution a fresh start.

The Revolution in Texas

The Mexican revolution had touched off a similar revolt in Texas. Led by Captain Juan Bautista de Las Casas, Spanish soldiers called for independence. They captured Texas governor Manuel María de Salcedo, the nephew of the commandant general, and put him in jail. But Las Casas's arrogance and his policies, as historian Wallace L. McKeehan wrote, "began to appear no different than the royalists that he had overturned."

Eventually, a group of people opposed to Las Casas gathered around a new leader—Lieutenant Colonel Juan Manuel Zambrano. Loyal to Ferdinand VII, these men overthrew Las Casas and executed him. Governor Salcedo and his supporters were released from prison. Soon afterward, they intercepted Father Hidalgo and his followers heading northward. Hidalgo and his men were quickly tried and shot by a firing squad in 1811.

Before Hidalgo's capture, however, he had sent a diplomat north to the United States. The revolutionaries hoped to receive military aid from President James Madison against the Spanish. José Bernardo Gutiérrez de Lara was chosen to travel to Washington, D.C. Although he failed to receive any aid from the U.S. government, Gutiérrez developed another plan. He met Anglos who were willing to join a small army to capture Texas. Together they formed the Republican Army of the North. Second in command was William Magee, an officer in the U.S. Army,

The town of San Antonio Texas in the 1800s.

who had resigned to lead the troops. In 1812, they crossed into Texas, quickly capturing the small presidio at Nacogdoches. Next, they marched westward and took control of the settlement at La Bahìa. But by this time, Governor Salcedo had advanced with an army of 1,500 men that besieged the town. Gutiérrez refused to surrender the city, although he lost Magee, who died during the siege. Salcedo eventually retreated toward San Antonio, the Texas capital.

JOSÉ BERNARDO GUTIÉRREZ

Born in 1774, José Bernardo Gutiérrez grew up in Revilla, Texas. His family was among the founders of the town. His father, Don Santiago Gutiérrez de Lara, owned a large rancho stretching for thousands of acres. As a young man, José Bernardo participated in expeditions against the Apache, who were raiding Texas during the 1790s.

In 1810, he joined the Mexican revolution. By this time, he had inherited his father's estates and become a wealthy man. Gutiérrez began his revolutionary activities by delivering pamphlets in east Texas calling for a revolt. Then he was asked by the revolutionary leaders to raise a force of soldiers. And before being captured, Father Hidalgo decided to send Gutiérrez to the United States to seek military assistance in the revolution.

Gutiérrez began a four-month journey, taking him through the Neutral Ground to Natchez, Mississippi. From there he traveled to Nashville, Tennessee. Along the way, he stayed at the homes of well-to-do Americans who supported the revolution. Eventually, Gutiérrez reached Washington, D.C., where he met with the secretary of war, William Eustis. He also spoke with the secretary of state, James Monroe. Secretary Monroe told Gutiérrez that Texas was part of the United States. He wanted U.S. troops to cross the border from Louisiana and take control of the area. But Gutiérrez said that he could not participate in such an expedition.

By the time he left Washington, D.C., Gutiérrez had received no help from the United States. He eventually headed southward, reaching New Orleans in March 1812. There he met with American diplomat William Shaler, a supporter of the revolution. From New Orleans, Shaler and Gutiérrez headed westward to Natchitoches, Louisiana. Once in Natchitoches, Gutiérrez met with Americans who favored a Mexican invasion of Texas. As a result, he began an effort to recapture Texas from Governor Salcedo.

The governor was pursued by the Army of the North, which rapidly advanced toward the capital. Outside the city, they defeated Salcedo's army in March 1813. Historian Randolph Campbell wrote, "Samuel Kemper, a native of Virginia who replaced Magee as military commander, led the charge that broke the royalists' line."

After the Army of the North entered San Antonio, Governor Salcedo and some of his political supporters were arrested. A group of soldiers, led by lieutenant Antonio Delgado, were ordered to guard them. Instead, the soldiers took Salcedo and his associates out of the city and, using swords, beheaded them. Then Delgado returned to the city, boasting of the murders. The Americans who had joined the Army of the North, including Kemper, were so upset by this that they left Texas.

This was only the beginning of Gutiérrez's problems. Although he had declared the independence of Texas in April 1813, his position was very uncertain. William Shaler, who had joined the Army of the North, refused to support Gutiérrez after the murders. Along with other Americans, Shaler began an effort to replace Gutiérrez. By August, Gutiérrez had been forced out of Texas. But by this time, the Spanish government in Mexico City had sent a large army north to Texas. Under the command of Colonel Joaquín de Arrendondo, the Spanish army easily defeated the Army of the North. Arrendondo then began rounding up the rebels and executing them. Many innocent people, including women and children, were sent to prison. Fearful of Arrendondo's reign of terror, hundreds of Texans fled the colony and crossed the border into Louisiana.

Mexican Independence

The independence movement had died in Texas. But inside Mexico, even after Hidalgo's death, rebels continued to operate against the Spanish government. In the north, Spain also confronted the threat from Anglos across the border in Louisiana. Spain feared they might launch another invasion with an even larger army. In 1819, this invasion occurred, led by a Natchez doctor named James Long. Long was upset by the Adams-Onis Treaty, signed in 1819. This treaty recognized Texas, west of the Sabine River, as part of the Spanish Empire. The United States had signed this agreement in return for receiving Florida, which had been a Spanish colony.

Long refused to accept the treaty, and led about three hundred men into Texas. They included men like James Bowie, a land speculator in Louisiana, and James Gaines, a ferry operator on the Sabine River. These men were called *filibusters*—from a Spanish word for people who defy authority. Long and his army of filibusters had the support of Gutiérrez, who was living in Louisiana. They captured Nacogdoches, just across the Texas border. Long then declared himself president of a newly independent Texas. A Spanish diplomat in New Orleans called Long's army the "most serious expedition that has threatened the Kingdom."

Mexican
filibusters on
the march to
reclaim land
in Texas.

But the success of the expedition lasted only a short time. The Spanish gathered an army of five hundred soldiers and soon drove Long's small army out of Texas. Unwilling to accept defeat, Long gathered another army and invaded Texas again. In 1821, he captured La Bahìa on the San Antonio River. It lay south of San Antonio, the capital of Texas. Once again, this was his only victory. Long and his men were soon captured by a superior Spanish army. Long was sent to prison in Mexico City, where he was killed by one of his guards.

By this time, Mexico City was no longer under the control of the Spanish. Another revolt had broken out, led by General Agustín de Iturbide, overthrowing the Spanish government. In 1821, Iturbide declared that Mexico had become independent, and the following year he became Emperor Agustín I, head of a new Mexican empire. A new flag rose over Texas, California, Arizona, and New Mexico, where Facundo Melgares served as governor. Now the Mexican government, instead of the Spanish, would be forced to deal with the threat from the United States. Long's invasion was only the beginning. More Anglos would follow. They would put increasing pressure on Texas, leading to another struggle for independence.

General Agustín de Iturbide helped Mexico win its independence in the early 1800s.

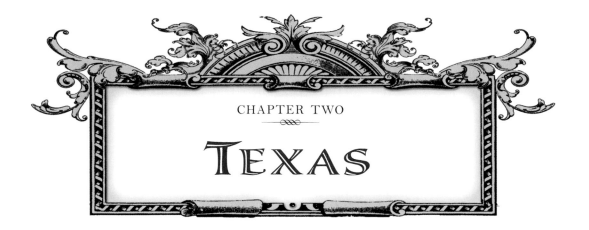

CHAPTER TWO

TEXAS

I N DECEMBER 1820, GOVERNOR ANTONIO
Martínez of Texas received a distinguished visitor in his
office at San Antonio. Moses Austin, gray-haired and
almost sixty, had been a successful mine owner and banker in
the Louisiana Territory. Louisiana had been part of the Spanish
empire from 1763 to 1800, before it was sold to France and later
to the United States. Austin had lost most of his money during
a recent economic downturn and went to San Antonio with a
new business proposal. He hoped to bring three hundred Anglo
families to Texas and establish a new settlement there.

At first Governor Martínez was not in favor of an Anglo
settlement. The Mexican government had recently been forced
to deal with filibusters invading Texas territory. But many
residents in San Antonio felt that Texas needed more settlers.

Opposite:
Anglo settlers
make their way
into Texas.

Hundreds had left because of the harsh rule of Colonel Arrendondo. In addition, influential political leaders who knew Austin told Martínez he would be the right man to establish such a settlement. So Governor Martínez finally agreed to Austin's request and asked the Mexican government to permit the settlers to enter Texas.

Moses Austin died in 1821, before he could return to settle in Texas. But when he was near death, he decided to have his son Stephen take over the project. Stephen Austin received an enormous piece of land, about 15,000 square miles (38,850 square km). But that was only a small part of the vast territory of Texas. Located along the Brazos and Colorado rivers, the soil on Austin's land was very fertile. It was also cheap—for about thirty dollars, a settler received almost 4,500 acres (1,821 hectares). As a result, Stephen Austin had no trouble finding Anglos who wanted to live in his new settlement. He began bringing settlers to Texas in 1822. Before settlers could receive their land, however, they had to first agree to become Mexican citizens and join the Catholic Church once they arrived in Texas.

LIFE IN THE MEXICAN EMPIRE

In 1824, Mexico established a new constitution that gave increased power to its states. Under the constitution, the Anglo settlers hoped that Texas would become a separate state with its own governor. But they were disappointed. There were too few people living in Texas. Instead, the

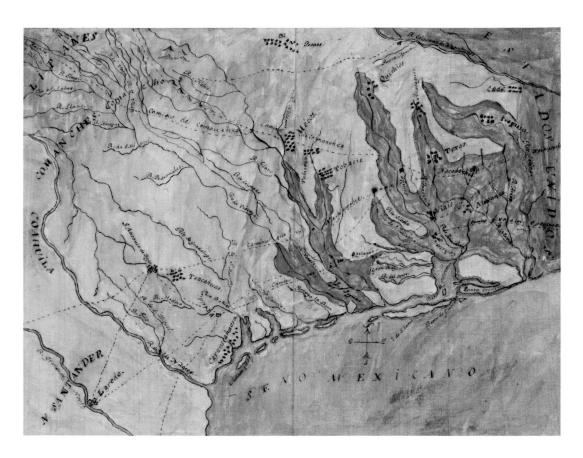

Mexican legislators decided to combine Texas with the much larger state of Coahuila, lying to the south. The new state, Coahuila y Texas, was governed from the town of Saltillo in Coahuila.

Many of the settlers who came to Texas were slave owners. Slavery in Texas was legal at that time. The settlers wanted slaves to plant cotton on the fertile lands that lay along the Brazos River. They sold their cotton, as well as the cattle they raised on huge ranches, to merchants in New Orleans. Mexicans living in Coahuila y Texas also began growing

Stephen Austin created this map of eastern Texas in 1822 to show where the settlements were. Prairie land is in yellow and woodland is in green.

cotton and shipping it to what was then the United States. The trade was very profitable because the Mexican government did not tax it.

During the 1820s, more Anglo settlers came to Texas. By 1825, Austin's settlement had reached almost 2,500 people. The Mexican government also granted permission to other Anglos to establish settlements. Although Texas was part of Coahuila, it had very little voice in the state legislature. But most *Texians*—as they were called—were accustomed to living on the frontier and defending themselves. Indeed, the Anglos formed their own *militias* to protect their homes in case of attacks by Native Americans.

In 1826, settlers from the settlement of Fredonia decided that they no longer wanted to be part of Coahuila y Texas and declared its independence. Austin did not support this effort, and, in 1827, these settlers were eventually driven out of Texas by the Mexican army. They were, "A small party of infatuated madmen," as Randolph Campbell wrote in *Gone to Texas*. Texians wanted to run their own affairs, independent of Mexico. Indeed, the Anglo immigrants often tended to look down on Mexicans—treating them as inferiors because of their brown skin.

While conflicts were occurring in Texas, violence had also broken out in central Mexico. The army revolted against the newly elected president, Gómez Pedraza, and refused to let him take office. Led by General Antonio

After his father's death, Stephen Austin continued to bring more Anglo families into Texas.

López de Santa Anna, the soldiers supported another candidate. General Santa Anna was a prominent criollo, who had already played a key role in Mexican politics. During the early 1820s, he and his soldiers had helped establish a republic. After the birth of the republic, Santa Anna became the governor of Yucatán on the east coast of Mexico. The state of Yucatán was located in the same area as Santa Anna's home in Veracruz.

With Santa Anna's help, Vicente Guerrero, the leader in the Mexican War of Independence became the new president of Mexico. In 1829, Guerrero and the Mexican legislature established a new law ending slavery in Mexico. The law was strongly opposed by the Anglo settlers in Texas. By this date, their population had grown to just over 20,000—many times the number of Mexicans living in Texas. To prevent conflict, the Mexican government allowed the Anglo planters to keep their slaves. But the planters were afraid that eventually they would be forced to free them.

CONFLICTS IN TEXAS

The enormous number of Anglo settlers in Texas was causing great concern in the Mexican government. In 1827, General José Manuel Rafael Simeón de Mier y Terán was sent north to Texas to report on conditions there.

Based on General Mier y Terán's report, the Mexican foreign relations minister, Lucas Alamán, prepared a new law. Passed by Congress in 1830, it became known as the

JOSÉ MANUEL RAFAEL SIMEÓN DE MIER Y TERÁN

Born in Mexico City in 1789, José Manuel Rafael Simeón de Mier y Terán participated in the Mexican War of Independence and helped establish the new republic. Becoming a brigadier general in 1824, he also served as minister of war in the Mexican Cabinet. With his military and mining background, Mier y Terán seemed a good choice to lead an expedition to Texas.

His mission was to report on the natural resources in the colony and the mood among the Anglo settlers. Leaving Mexico City in November 1827, Mier y Terán traveled in a magnificent coach, decorated with silver. Along with him were a mapmaker and an artist who had come to chart the area. General Mier y Terán praised the successful farms and ranches that had been established by the Anglo settlers. But he also feared that another revolt might occur.

In his report to the government, Mier y Terán mentioned that the settlers were "troublemakers," who created an "uproar" in Texas. Although they had promised to be loyal to Mexico and become Catholics, the settlers had violated these promises. Mier y Terán urged that President Guerrero send more Mexican troops to the area. He also suggested that the government bring Mexican colonists into Texas. After returning to Mexico City, Mier y Terán joined Santa Anna in defending Mexico from a Spanish invasion. The Spanish wanted to bring Mexico back into their empire. But they were defeated at Tampico, on the east coast, in 1829.

Soon afterward, Mier y Terán became commandant general of Texas y Coahuila. Meanwhile, Anglo immigration continued, and Mexico was caught up in another civil war. Mier y Terán became very depressed over these events. "We are lost," he said. "Texas is lost. What will become of Texas?" His health had also become very poor. As a result, he killed himself with his own sword in 1832.

Law of April 6, 1830. It called for an end to Anglo immigration into Texas. In addition, no more slaves would be allowed to enter, and Anglos would not be permitted to trade with the United States. Texians were furious over the new law. Stephen Austin said the impact would be "fatal" on future relations between Texas and Mexico. Mier y Terán was put in charge of the troops being sent to Texas. He recognized how angry the Anglo settlers felt over the new law. He urged the Mexican government not to outlaw slavery, and he allowed those settlers on their way to Texas to cross the border.

Nevertheless, relations between the Mexican government and the settlers in Texas continued to grow worse. The Texians were especially upset because the Law of April 6, 1830 called for the collection of taxes on goods that they were selling outside of Mexico. These taxes, known as customs duties, would cut into the profits of Texian merchants. The Mexican government established a collection office for customs payments at Anahuac on the Texas Gulf Coast. Customs were collected here on all ships leaving or entering the major port of Galveston.

In December 1831, a Texian ship tried to leave the coast without paying these duties. A battle broke out with Mexican officials who tried to stop it.

As a result, Anáhuac became a center of Texian opposition to the new laws. Among its leaders was a lawyer named William Travis. He had just moved to Anahuac from

A political cartoon from the 1800s showing those burdened by the taxes imposed by government (left) contrasted to those who did not have to pay taxes (right).

Alabama in 1831. The bearded, heavyset Travis hoped to start a new life after his business interests in Alabama had failed. Travis constantly clashed with the Mexican authorities, led by Juan Davis Bradburn—commander at Anahuac. Bradburn believed that the customs duties should be collected. Since slavery had been abolished in Mexico, he also believed that any runaway slaves who came to Texas from the United States should remain free. Travis disagreed, and he gave his support to a new militia group organized by the Anglos to oppose Bradburn. In 1832, Bradburn put Travis in prison, because he was a ringleader of the Anglos. But he was later freed by the Mexican authorities.

CIVIL WAR IN MEXICO AND TEXAS

Meanwhile, civil war had broken out once again in central Mexico. The struggle involved President Anastasio Bustamante and General Santa Anna. Bustamante favored more power for the president and less freedom for the Mexican states. Santa Anna wanted to give the states more independence. The Texians supported Santa Anna because it meant that they would have more control over their own government. In 1832, a Texian militia attacked the Mexican *garrison*, which supported the Bustamante government, at Nacogdoches near the Louisiana border. Led by Colonel José de las Piedras, the Mexican soldiers tried to defend Nacogdoches. Fierce house-to-house fighting broke out between Piedras's men and the Texian militia. Eventually Piedras retreated, after more than thirty of his men were killed.

Antonio López de Santa Anna fought to make Mexico independent from Texas.

The militia, led by James Bowie, went after Piedras and his army. Several years earlier, Bowie had participated in the filibuster invasion led by James Long. Afterward, he had become a friend of Stephen Austin, who sent him to Nacogdoches. Bowie chased Piedras and eventually trapped him, forcing his soldiers to surrender.

TOWARD INDEPENDENCE

Texians did not stop the drive for independence with the defeat of Colonel Piedras. Encouraged by their success, they selected delegates from across the territory to meet at San Felipe de Austin in October 1832. The delegates elected Stephen Austin as president of the convention. They drafted a series of resolutions, calling for the Mexican government to permit immigration into Texas and to end the customs duties. The delegates also wanted permission to create their own militias. Once the convention was completed, the resolutions were sent to Mexico City. At the capital, meanwhile, President Bustamante had been driven out of office. Early in 1833, Santa Anna was elected president of the republic.

In April, Texians met at another convention in San Felipe de Austin. This time they prepared a stronger series of resolutions, which they planned to submit to President Santa Anna. Among the most prominent delegates at the convention was Sam Houston—a former governor of Tennessee and U.S. congressman, who had immigrated to Texas. Houston believed that constant civil war in Mexico meant that Texas needed to govern itself. He and other delegates called for Texas to become an independent state within Mexico, with its own government separate from Coahuila y Texas. They asked Austin to travel to Mexico City and present these resolutions to President Santa Anna.

The new president had seemed to be a strong believer in

federalism—more power for the states, and less for the central government. But when he received the Texian resolutions, Santa Anna was outraged. The president felt that the Texas conventions had been illegal. He also realized that if the Texian demands were met, this might lead to revolts in other Mexican states. Santa Anna and Austin held a meeting in Mexico City late in 1833. The president said he would consider the Texian resolutions. However, Austin had already been telling his colleagues in Texas to establish an independent state. Santa Anna was furious when he heard what Austin had done; and in January 1834, Austin was arrested.

William Travis was a lawyer who clashed with Mexican authorities.

Texians became very angry when they heard of Austin's imprisonment. Led by William Travis and others, they decided to go ahead with plans to set up a state government. The Anglos were supported by many *Tejanos*—Mexicans living in Texas.

Late in 1834, Austin was released from prison. Meanwhile, Santa Anna had taken more power into his own hands. Revolts began to break out in several Mexican states that supported greater federalism. But the rebel groups were defeated by Santa Anna's army. In Texas, however, the revolt continued to spread. Texians were outraged at Santa Anna for reducing the power of the other states. William Travis called Santa

JUAN SEGUÍN

Among the leading Tejanos was Juan Seguín, the *alcalde* (mayor) of San Antonio. Born in 1806, Seguín was a member of a prominent family who had been among the early settlers of San Antonio. In 1825, Seguín married Maria Gertrudis Flores de Abrego, and the couple had ten children. Seguín later pursued a political career in Texas. He became an alderman in 1828 and was elected alcalde in 1833. Seguín believed that President Santa Anna was not truly a supporter of federalism, but wanted to rule Mexico as a dictator. In 1835, Seguín became a captain in the revolutionary Army of Texas and fought against the Mexicans during the war of independence. That same year, Seguín was involved in the battle at San Antonio and served at the Alamo. However, before the Alamo was surrounded by Santa Anna's army, Seguín had been sent out to find reinforcements. The following year, Captain Juan Seguín led the only Tejano unit at the Battle of San Jacinto. After Texas gained independence, Seguín would be the only Tejano to serve in the senate of the new republic. During the 1840s, he was elected mayor of San Antonio, but his conflicts with the Anglo settlers eventually led Seguín to leave San Antonio for Mexico. Seguín served in the Mexican War during the 1840s, fighting against the U.S. forces that invaded Mexico. Eventually, he would return to Texas, where he died in 1890.

Anna's administration a "plundering, robbing, autocratical, aristocratical, jumbled up government which is in fact no government at all," wrote William Davis in *Three Roads to the Alamo*.

The symbol of that government was the customs house at Anahuac, under the command of Captain Antonio Tenorio. The Mexicans continued to collect customs duties, angering the Texian merchants. In June 1835, Travis and a few other men decided to drive the Mexicans out of Anahuac. They sailed a small ship across Galveston Bay, and fired a cannon at the town. Then they demanded that Tenorio surrender. When he refused, Travis attacked the town and took control of it.

A similar event occurred in Nacogdoches. In July, James Bowie and other Texians took over a Mexican supply depot that was filled with guns and ammunition. Many Texians now waited, expecting Santa Anna to strike back. Stephen Austin believed that war with Mexico could begin at any moment. "We must rely on ourselves and prepare for the worst," he said.

MEXICO AND TEXAS AT WAR

Santa Anna had no intention of permitting Texas to continue its revolt. In July 1835, he sent General Martín Perfecto de Cos north from Mexico City to take command of Mexican troops in Texas. Cos was thirty-six, with dark hair and a black moustache. A relative of Santa Anna, he had risen rapidly in the army, becoming a brigadier general in 1833. Cos reached

Goliad, formerly called La Bahía, near the Texas coast in October, and from there headed north to San Antonio. Cos was expected to arrest Travis and put an immediate end to the revolt in Texas. But before Cos had even arrived, a battle had already broken out at Gonzales, east of San Antonio. A Mexican force, under the command of Francisco de Castañeda, had been driven off by a superior Texian army. As Stephen Austin put it, "War is declared." Shortly afterward, Austin began to form the Army of Texas, intending to march on San Antonio.

Martín Perfecto de Cos commanded Mexican troops in Texas.

As General Cos reached San Antonio, news arrived of another Texian victory. A small force had marched on Goliad, attacked the Presidio La Bahía, and captured the town. With Goliad in Texian hands, the Mexican army in San Antonio could not receive supplies from the coast. In the meantime, Austin and his army were advancing toward the Mexican garrison in San Antonio. But Cos had no intention of giving up the city to the Texian rebels. He said to his soldiers, "These ungrateful men have revolted against our government, and assumed the right to live as they like, without any subjection to the laws of the republic."

The Mexican soldiers prepared to defend the city. Many of them were stationed in an old mission called the Alamo. They had placed cannons on the walls to drive off Austin and his army. Austin planned to surround San Antonio, cut off supplies coming into the city, and force Cos to surrender. He had placed James Bowie in charge of the advance units of the army. As they approached San Antonio, General Cos launched an attack against Bowie's soldiers. A fierce battle broke out amid the fog that lay along a nearby river. Mexican cannons fired at the Texians, trying to drive them back. But Bowie ordered repeated charges, forcing the Mexican soldiers off the field and back into San Antonio.

As Austin approached the city, important events were occurring elsewhere. Texas political leaders were meeting in San Felipe. Under the leadership of Sam Houston, they decided to set up a Texas government. But they did not declare their independence from Mexico. Nevertheless, they selected Houston to organize volunteers who were arriving in Texas from the United States. Among them was a unit from Louisiana known as the New Orleans Greys. They had heard about the situation in Texas and came to help the Texians resist the Mexican armies.

In the meantime, Cos and his army of several hundred men prepared to defend themselves. On December 5, they faced an attack led by Colonel Benjamin Milam. With three hundred men, including the New Orleans Greys, Milam fought a house-to-house battle against the Mexicans. Cos

A scene
from the battle
at the Alamo.

directed his cannons against the advancing Texians in the
streets of San Antonio. Mexican cannon fire also thundered
from the walls of the Alamo. Two days later, the battle was still
raging, but Milam and his men were gaining ground. The
Mexicans were gradually driven out of the houses which they

had been trying to defend. Finally, on December 9, 1833, General Cos surrendered. The Mexicans were allowed to leave San Antonio, after promising they would not participate in the rest of the war.

BATTLES FOR VICTORY

While the battle was still raging in San Antonio, General Santa Anna was marching northward with an army of about 6,000 soldiers. Dressed in white pants and blue coats with red lapels, the soldiers left San Luis Potosí, Mexico in December 1835. Santa Anna regarded Texas as a critical territory for Mexico. Unless the revolt was put down, he worried that other Mexican states might join it. He also feared that U.S. citizens might pour into the area if Texas were lost. From there, they might try to take over other Mexican territories in Arizona, New Mexico, and California.

When news arrived that Santa Anna was marching toward Texas, the Texians knew that he would try to retake San Antonio. Under the leadership of William Travis and James Bowie, they decided to fortify themselves inside the Alamo.

William Travis
(left), musters
his men during
the siege of
the Alamo.

Fewer than two hundred men defended the old Spanish mission. They included Anglos, such as the frontiersman David (Davy) Crockett. Among the defenders, there was also a group of Tejanos led by Juan Seguín. "We pledged ourselves to use all our influence to rouse Texas against the tyrannical government of Santa Anna," he later wrote. But as Santa Anna approached the fortress, Seguín was sent on a mission to Goliad to bring reinforcements.

By early March, Santa Anna had surrounded the Alamo. In the meantime, Texas political leaders were meeting at Washington-on-the-Brazos, northeast of San Antonio. On March 2, they declared Texas an independent republic. Santa Anna hoped to bring an end to Texas independence as soon as possible. Instead of surrounding the Alamo with his vast army, he decided to attack the fortress. Before dawn on March 6, he ordered his men to storm the walls of the Alamo. They were led by General Cós, who had returned to the battlefield after his defeat at San Antonio. Although hundreds of Mexican soldiers fell dead or wounded during the attack, they eventually brought their scaling ladders to the walls of the Alamo. There were too few Texians to stop them. Mexican soldiers swarmed over the tops of the walls, and fierce hand-to-hand fighting broke out. Once inside, the Mexican soldiers killed almost all of the defenders.

In Goliad, Juan Seguín had gathered reinforcements to bring to the Alamo. But as he approached, he realized that Santa Anna's army had taken over the fortress. He was too late to do the Texians any good. Santa Anna's victory at the Alamo was followed by another triumph at Goliad in mid-March. Under the command of thirty-nine-year-old General José de Urrea, Mexican forces defeated the Texians. Santa Anna ordered that all the captive soldiers be executed. "These orders always seemed to me harsh," General Urrea said later in his published diary. But Urrea felt that he had no choice but to obey orders. "I was unable, therefore, to carry out the good intentions dictated by my feelings . . . overcome by the difficult circumstances that surrounded me. I authorized the execution . . . of thirty adventurers taken prisoners . . . setting free those who were colonists or Mexicans."

SAN JACINTO

Following the victories at Goliad and the Alamo, Santa Anna began marching east. He hoped to trap the army being formed by General Sam Houston. General Santa Anna divided his forces into three columns. One headed toward the coast, another trekked northward, and a third column headed toward San Felipe. As they marched eastward, Houston and his army retreated. By April 15, Santa Anna had reached Harrisburg. This had become the capital of the Texas republic. Santa Anna had hoped to capture the leaders of the new republic, but they fled before he arrived.

Still hoping to trap the Texas leaders and end the rebellion, Santa Anna took an army unit of five hundred men and rapidly marched after them. Houston received word that Santa Anna had divided his army. He decided that this decision presented an opportunity to defeat Santa Anna and possibly capture him. Both armies were heading toward the San Jacinto River. On April 20, as they both reached the river, a battle broke out along its banks. But neither side could win a victory, and both withdrew for the night. By morning, Santa Anna had been reinforced by another army unit commanded by General Cos. The Mexican army fortified its position, expecting an attack at any time. By late in the afternoon, however, when the Texas army did not advance, Santa Anna decided to rest his troops.

Houston's army finally attacked at about 4:00 p.m., catching Santa Anna's forces completely off guard. "Remember the Alamo," the Texians shouted, as they swarmed among the Mexican soldiers. In hand-to-hand combat lasting less than twenty minutes, Santa Anna's army was defeated. Although the Mexican soldiers threw down their rifles, Houston's men began to massacre them. Santa Anna escaped, but soon afterward, he was captured. "You have conquered the Napoleon of the West," he said. "You have whipped me, I am your prisoner," as historian William Davis wrote in *Lone Star Rising*.

Afraid for his life, Santa Anna decided to sign two agreements with the Texians. According to the first one, all his armies were to be withdrawn from Texas. In return

for his release, Santa Anna also made a secret agreement with Texas leaders. He promised to recognize the independence of Texas, known as the Lone Star Republic. Mexican armies retreated from Texas, and Santa Anna was later sent home to Veracruz. The war was over, and Mexico had lost an important part of its empire.

Santa Anna's troops rest in Harris County, Texas.

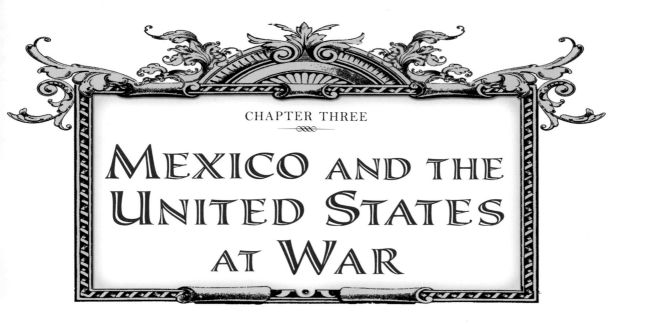

CHAPTER THREE

Mexico and the United States at War

A FTER THE STRUGGLE OVER TEXAS HAD ended, Juan Seguín and other Tejanos found themselves in an unfamiliar situation. Suddenly they had become residents of a new nation—the Lone Star Republic. Seguín also discovered that Tejanos had become second-class citizens. As historian William Davis wrote, "Anglos slowly began to freeze them out, challenging or revoking their land titles, denying their election to office, and even threatening their lives." Before much longer, Seguín and other Tejanos left the Texas republic to live in Mexico.

Meanwhile, the Mexican government refused to accept the agreements made by Santa Anna after the Battle of San Jacinto. Mexican political leaders still regarded Texas as part

Opposite:
The original color design sketch for the Republic of Texas flag.

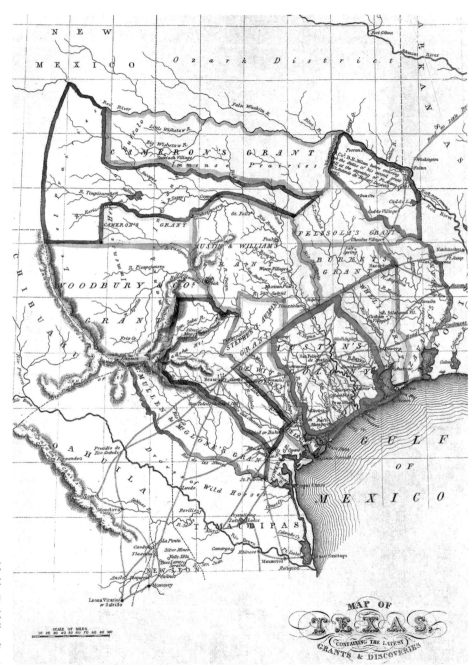

A map showing the earliest settlements in Texas, during its first year of independence in 1836.

of Mexico. Conflicts broke out along the border, and Mexico mounted an unsuccessful invasion of San Antonio in 1842.

The Lone Star Republic remained independent from 1836 until 1845 because of slavery: Northerners were opposed to another slave state joining the United States. During this period, Texas was recognized as a separate government by the United States and Great Britain. In 1841, Texan leaders tried to expand their republic by sending an expedition into New Mexico to take over part of its territory. Since the early 1820s, traders from Missouri had been traveling hundreds of miles to Santa Fe to conduct business. Known as the Santa Fe Trail, this became a lucrative trading route. Anglo traders brought merchandise, such as cotton, to trade for gold and silver that was mined in Arizona and New Mexico. Texans hoped to take control of the Santa Fe Trail by conquering New Mexico.

A group of merchants carrying $200,000 in trade goods left Texas in June 1841. Along with them was a small army of nearly three hundred men, led by Hugh McCleod. After dealing with Native-American attacks and losing their way, the expedition finally arrived in New Mexico. But they were met by Governor Manuel Armijo, who convinced them to surrender. Afterward, they were sent to prison in Mexico City, although the Mexican authorities eventually freed them.

Steps Toward War

Most residents of Texas wanted to become part of the United States. Various efforts were made to push a bill through Congress, making Texas a state. However, it was strongly opposed by northern congressmen. If Texas entered the Union, it would become a slave state. Northerners were fiercely against adding another slave state that might make the South more powerful. By 1845, however, there was enough support to admit Texas as the twenty-eighth state in the Union. But bringing Texas into the United States led to a furious outcry in Mexico. Mexican leaders still considered Texas part of Mexico. They charged that the United States had no authority to take over Mexican territory.

However, U.S. president James K. Polk not only supported the admission of Texas to the Union but also wanted other parts of Mexico as well. Polk believed that California would give the United States important harbors on the west coast to promote trade with the Far East. The president also wanted to add the New Mexico territory to the United States. He supported the Texas claim that its state boundary should be expanded. Texans demanded that the Rio Grande River be considered the southern boundary of the state, not the Nueces River.

In 1845, President Polk sent an ambassador, John Slidell, to Mexico City to purchase these new territories for the United States. Once Mexicans heard that Slidell was coming,

President James K. Polk, the eleventh president of the United States, supported the admission of Texas to the Union.

they were furious. They suspected that the Mexican president, José Joaquín de Herrera, might be planning to make a deal. The Mexican army, commanded by General Mariano Paredes, overthrew Herrera, and Paredes took power.

War Begins

With negotiations going nowhere in Mexico, President Polk had already taken matters into his own hands. During the summer of 1845, he had directed an army of 1,500 soldiers to the Nueces River. This small force was commanded by sixty-one-year-old General Zachary Taylor. General Taylor was a veteran of the War of 1812 against Great Britain, and an activist in campaigns against the Seminole Indian tribe. Early in 1846, Taylor was ordered to continue southward to the banks of the Rio Grande. The troops advanced, accompanied by a full marching band. By this time, Taylor's army had grown to over 3,500 soldiers. When they reached the Rio Grande, they began building a fort directly across the river from the Mexican town of Matamoros. President Polk hoped to provoke an attack on American troops, so he could tell the U.S. Congress that the Mexicans had started a war.

In April, the Mexican garrison was reinforced by an army of 3,000 soldiers under the command of General Pedro de Ampudia. Born in Cuba in 1803, Ampudia had fought alongside Santa Anna at the Alamo. Named general in chief of the Army of the North in 1846, he was considered a cruel man and not well liked by the Mexican residents of

Matamoros. They wanted him replaced with a much more popular general, Mariano Arista, who arrived soon afterward. The Mexicans regarded the American fort as a threat to Matamoros and wanted it removed. In late April, a brief skirmish occurred between Mexican and U.S. cavalries along the Rio Grande. General Taylor immediately sent a short message to President Polk telling him that "Hostilities may now be considered as commenced." Polk then declared war on Mexico.

In the meantime, General Arista crossed the Rio Grande. His force was larger than Taylor's army. Arista threatened to capture the U.S. supply depot, located east of the river. Taylor retreated, gathered his supplies, and then headed back to the Rio Grande. The two armies clashed at Palo Alto on May 8, 1846. Arista opened the battle by firing his artillery at Taylor's infantry. The U.S. troops answered the bombardment and proved far more effective, killing many Mexican soldiers. Although Arista launched his cavalry in successive waves against the U.S. infantry, he could not force the Americans from the battlefield. By the end of the day, neither side had won a

General Pedro de Ampudia commanded the Mexican army beginning in 1846.

victory. Arista retreated by the next morning. The Battle of Resaca de la Palma broke out on May 9, and this time the Mexicans were driven from the battlefield. Arista retreated across the Rio Grande and abandoned the town of Matamoros.

BATTLE AT MONTERREY

After he was defeated in Texas, General Arista was replaced by Pedro de Ampudia, who became head of the Army of the North. The army had received reinforcements, increasing its size to about 10,000 soldiers. Ampudia marched into Monterrey in northern Mexico where he hoped to stop Taylor's army. But Taylor was determined to advance through northern Mexico and take control of it.

Late in September, General Taylor's army, numbering about 12,000, approached Monterrey. The city was heavily protected by massive forts, with cannons covering the walls. Ampudia expected that they

The Battle of Monterrey, depicted here, took place in Monterrey, Mexico in 1846.

could easily withstand any assault. For three days in September a battle raged around Monterrey. American artillery men lobbed hundreds of shells into the Mexican *citadels*. Although the Mexican forces tried to hold out, their positions were stormed by American troops, who pushed their way into the center of the city. By September 25, Ampudia had raised the white flag in surrender.

Mexico's armies seemed unable to win a victory that would stop the U.S. invasion. Although the Mexican soldiers were courageous in battle, they lacked good equipment and effective leadership. But the nation's political leaders turned to someone they hoped might change the situation— Antonio López de Santa Anna. General Santa Anna had held the presidency during the 1840s, but he had been driven from office because of corruption. Now the Mexican people wanted him back.

BATTLE AT BUENA VISTA

Santa Anna quickly headed north, raising an army of over 23,000 at San Luis Potosí. He marched northward, approaching General Taylor's army at a mountain pass called Buena Vista. American forces numbered only about one-third of the Mexican troops. Blessed by priests who had accompanied the expedition, the Mexican forces attacked during the early morning of February 23, 1847. United States infantry troops occupying the hills around the pass were driven back. At one point, one of Taylor's commanders told him, "General, we are whipped." But Taylor replied, "This is for me to determine,"as John S.D. Eisenhower wrote in *So Far From God*. His troops stiffened their defenses and pushed back Santa Anna's forces. The Mexicans were unable to win a victory and lost almost six hundred soldiers. The next day, Santa Anna retreated from the battlefield and returned to Mexico City.

BATTLES IN THE WEST

While the war was raging in Texas and northern Mexico, a campaign was also under way farther west. President Polk had sent a small army of 1,600 men commanded by Colonel Stephen Kearny to New Mexico and California. His mission was to bring these two territories under the control of the United States. Americans regarded the possession of New Mexico and California as part of their *Manifest Destiny*. This term is used to describe the belief that Americans had a special destiny to expand its territory over all of North America.

By the 1840s, the population of New Mexico numbered over 40,000. The capital, Santa Fe, was the target of Kearny's expedition. The governor of New Mexico, Manuel Armijo, had assembled a small army to defend the area. A heavyset man, about fifty-three years old, Armijo had defended New Mexico during the Texas invasion several years earlier. But this time Armijo seemed afraid to fight. As Kearny approached, the governor left Santa Fe without trying to

Brigadier
General
Stephen Watts
Kearny captures
Santa Fe, New
Mexico in
August 1846.

stop the invasion. As a result, Kearny's troops easily entered the capital and took over New Mexico in August 1846.

Even before Kearny reached New Mexico, war had broken out in California. By the 1840s, the territory had only a few settlers. They included about 1,000 Mexican residents, called *Californios*. The Californios raised cattle and grew citrus fruits, such as oranges and lemons. Several small settlements had arisen in California. Los Angeles had a population of about 250 people, while about 100 lived in San Diego. There were 700 residents in both Monterey and San José. Small communities had also been established at San Francisco and Sacramento. The southern part of California was directed by Governor Pío Pico in Los Angeles. General José Castro ran northern California from Monterey. A few U.S. settlers had also moved to California, many of them living around Sutter's Fort. This settlement had been established by John Sutter along the Sacramento River on a large stretch of land given to him by the Mexican government.

Early in 1846, General Castro encountered an expedition led by an American explorer named John C. Frémont. Captain Frémont said that he had come to California to explore a route to Oregon. But Castro was suspicious of Frémont's mission and eventually told him to leave the area. Although Frémont headed north to Oregon, he returned to California in the spring. He had received a secret message from the U.S. government. The contents of the message were never made public, but they seemed to indicate that Frémont and his men might have an important role to play in making California part of the United States. By the time he returned to California, American settlers had taken control of a small settlement at Sonoma. They declared that California was an independent republic. Frémont took command of the men at Sonoma, planning to take California from the Mexican government.

Before Frémont could begin his campaign, however, Monterey had already been captured. Commodore John Sloat, commanding the U.S. Pacific Squadron, had entered Monterey harbor in July. General Castro, who had been defending the city, retreated to Los Angeles. In August, this settlement also fell to U.S. forces, who later took San Diego. The Californios tried to regroup and push the American troops out of California. For a brief period in late 1846, they succeeded in driving U.S. troops out of Los Angeles and San Diego. But late in the year, Colonel Kearny arrived in California, and by early 1847, Kearny and his troops had defeated the Californios.

American explorer John C. Frémont came to California in order to explore a route to Oregon.

INVASION OF MEXICO

Soon afterward, the war began to enter its final phases. A large U.S. force, consisting of about 8,600 troops, landed on the Mexican coast. Their first target was the port of Veracruz, under the command of General Juan Morales and with about 3,400 Mexican soldiers. The American army, commanded by General Winfield Scott, pounded the walls of Veracruz with heavy artillery. Hundreds of people inside the city walls were killed or wounded. But Scott would not allow any civilians to leave. Finally, after

Mexican soldiers at the outset of the war with the United States in 1846.

JOSÉ MARIÁ FLORES

Born in Mexico in 1818, José Flores later joined the Mexican army. He was ordered to California in 1842, where he served under General Castro. After Los Angeles surrendered to U.S. forces, Lieutenant Archibald Gillespie was put in command of the city. Soon afterward, he arrested twenty Californios after receiving reports that they planned to overthrow the new government. Other Californios asked Captain Flores, who had remained in Los Angeles, to lead a revolt against the Americans. Gathering a small force, Flores forced Gillespie and his soldiers to leave Los Angeles in February 1846. Following his success at Los Angeles, Flores ordered some of his men to recapture other towns that had fallen to the Americans. They took Santa Barbara and San Diego. With only about two hundred men and few weapons, Flores regained control of California. In November 1846, he became governor of the territory. But early the next year, Colonel Stephen Kearny and Commodore Robert Stockton launched an attack on the Flores government. On January 8, 1847, they defeated Flores at the Battle of Rio San Gabriel outside Los Angeles. On January 12, the Californios surrendered to the U.S. forces. Flores left California and returned to Mexico, dying in 1866.

a twelve-day bombardment, the Mexicans surrendered on March 27, 1847.

American forces then headed inland toward Mexico City. Santa Anna tried to halt the advance at Cerro Gordo, about halfway to the capital. But his army was driven from their defenses and forced to retreat. By summer, General Scott had reached the outskirts of Mexico City. After a series of bloody battles, American forces finally captured the city in September 1847.

Following their defeat, Mexican leaders agreed to peace with the United States. At Guadalupe Hidalgo, outside Mexico City, U.S. ambassador Nicholas Trist signed a peace agreement with Mexican leaders. Under the terms of the treaty, Mexico lost about half its territory in 1848. California, Nevada, Utah, and parts of Colorado, Arizona, New Mexico, and Wyoming became part of the United States. In return, the Mexican government received about 18 million dollars. Mexico also agreed to recognize the Rio Grande River as the Texas border.

The lives of all the Mexicans living in these territories had changed forever.

CHAPTER FOUR

NO PEACE FOR MEXICAN AMERICANS

BEFORE THE WAR BETWEEN MEXICO AND the United States, the family of José de los Reyes Berreyessa had been prominent Californios. They owned large ranchos with cattle and horses. But as the war began in 1846, American immigrants in California murdered Berreyessa and his two nephews. Nicolás Berreyessa, another member of the large family, lost a herd of horses that was stolen from his ranch by Anglos. They also entered his home and stole many of his valuable possessions.

As the war ended, the lives of the Berreyessa family changed even more. In 1848, gold was discovered at Sutter's settlement. During the following year, as many as 90,000 people came to California to stake out claims and enrich themselves with gold.

Opposite:
U.S. General
Winfield Scott
and his army
enter Mexico City
in 1847, during
the Mexican-
American War.

Some traveled overland from the east, while others came by ship. Although a few miners struck it rich, many others were disappointed and found little gold. They soon left the gold-fields to settle on fertile California land.

Some of this land belonged to the Berreyessa family. Although the Berreyessas went to court to preserve their property and keep settlers off it, they failed. Anglo judges, lawyers, and land surveyors said that the Californios did not have the proper titles to their lands. Many of their land deeds had been issued by the Spanish years earlier. The deeds were unclear and written in Spanish, which the Anglos did not understand. Therefore, they ruled that the property belonged to anyone who wanted to build a house on it.

Demesio Berreyessa was accused of killing an Anglo who tried to take his land. A lynch mob took Berreyessa from his home and hanged him without a trial. As Antonio Berreyessa later put it, "Of all the California families, perhaps ours can most justly complain about the bad faith of adventurers and squatters and about the illegal activities of the American lawyers."

But the experiences of the Berreyessa family were not unique. The Treaty of Guadalupe Hidalgo was supposed to protect the property rights of Mexicans whose land had become part of the United States. But these land rights were removed from the treaty by the U.S. Senate before ratification. As a result, in San José, California, for example, the government surveyor was an Anglo named William Lewis who had come out during the gold rush. He could not read Spanish and paid no attention to the land deeds of the Californios. Instead he turned their land over to the Anglo immigrants.

Lewis and others justified their actions by pointing out that the Californios had done nothing to improve their estates. Instead of plowing the fields and planting crops, they raised cattle and sheep. Anglos felt that most of the cattle and sheep herders were penniless Mexican peons or Native Americans. A local newspaper editor called the Californios a "nation of drones" who had no right to the land. Others looked down on the Californios because of their skin color. They believed the white race was superior. As author Thomas Jefferson Farnham explained, "The Californians are an imbecile . . . race of men, and unfit to control the destinies of that beautiful country."

Many Californio families spent large amounts of money on legal expenses trying to defend their property rights in court. In the end, they generally lost their land. As a result,

A portrait of a typical Californio.

many Mexican families were forced to go to work for the Anglos who had taken over their property. They took jobs as herders and farm workers. A few, however, turned to illegal methods of earning money. For example, during the 1850s an outlaw named Joaquin Murieta robbed Anglo businesses until he was finally captured and killed in 1853.

According to legend, Murieta had begun his life of crime after failing to make a living in the California goldfields. Many Mexicans had come to California, beginning in 1848, from the mining area of Sonora, Mexico. Once they reached California, however, the Mexicans ran into extreme racial prejudice from the Anglo miners. These men tried to drive the Mexicans out of the goldfields. The California government finally passed a twenty-dollar tax on miners who were not U.S. citizens. This was too much for the Mexican miners to afford, so they left the goldfields and took other jobs.

ARIZONA AND NEW MEXICO

Conditions for Mexican Americans were different in Arizona and New Mexico, however. New Mexico had a much larger population—about 70,000 Mexican Americans during the 1850s. Only a few Anglos moved into the area, so the racism that occurred in California did not exist in New Mexico.

In 1853, the territory of New Mexico and Arizona grew larger as a result of the U.S. purchase of more land from Mexico. President Franklin Pierce was interested in

After having a hard time trying to make a living in the California goldfields, Joaquin Murieta turned to illegal means of earning money.

NO PEACE FOR MEXICAN AMERICANS

The centenary of the Gadsden Purchase was commemorated by the United States Postal Service with a stamp in 1953.

a plan to build a transcontinental railroad from the east coast to California. A possible route for the railroad would take it through territory in northern Mexico. Pierce directed the U.S. ambassador to Mexico, James Gadsden, to meet with President Santa Anna about acquiring the territory. The Mexican government needed money after the war with the United States. So, for a price of 10 million dollars, Santa Anna agreed to sell the 29,000 square miles (75,110 square km) that formed the southern sections of present-day Arizona and New Mexico. This became known as the Gadsden Purchase. Nevertheless, Mexicans were so upset at losing even more territory to the United States that they drove Santa Anna from office. He never again became president of Mexico.

Manifest Destiny had brought California and the Southwest into the United States. For Mexican Americans, it meant becoming a minority. In the face of prejudice and misunderstanding, however, they would strive to preserve their customs, their traditions, and their religious beliefs. As a result, during the years ahead, Mexican Americans made important contributions to the culture of America.

TIMELINE

1803	United States makes Louisiana Purchase.
1806	Facundo Melgares leads expedition to stop Lewis and Clark.
1808	Spanish King Ferdinand VII overthrown by Napoleon.
1810	Revolution begins in Mexico to overthrow Spanish rule.
1813	Republican Army of the North takes control of Texas.
1819	Adams-Onis Treaty recognizes Texas as part of Mexico.
1819–1821	James Long leads invasions of Texas from Louisiana; Long is defeated.
1821	Mexico becomes an independent nation.
1822	Stephen Austin establishes new settlement in Texas.
1829	Mexico abolishes slavery, angering Texian slave owners.
1830	Mexican law closes off immigration to Texas.
1832	Convention of Texas settlers calls for Mexico to reopen immigration.
1834	Austin travels to Mexico City; imprisoned by President Santa Anna.
1835	Conflict breaks out between Mexican army and Texas immigrants.
1836	Texas War of Independence; battles at Alamo and San Jacinto; Texas becomes independent republic.
1836–1845	Lone Star Republic remains independent.
1841	Lone Star Republic launches unsuccessful invasion of New Mexico.
1845	Texas becomes part of the United States.
1846–1848	Mexican War fought between Mexico and United States.
1848	Treaty of Guadalupe Hidalgo ends war; United States acquires California and Southwest from Mexico.
1848	Gold is discovered in California; thousands of settlers rush into new territory, overwhelming Mexican Americans.
1853	Gadsden Purchase adds more Mexican territory to United States in Southwest.

Glossary

alcalde Mayor of a town in Mexico.

Anglos White Americans living in the Mexican empire.

Californios Mexican residents of California.

citadel A fortress used in defense during an attack or siege.

criollos Individuals of Spanish ancestry born in Mexico.

federalism A form of government in which political power is divided between the central government and the states.

filibusters Anglos in Texas who defied Spanish authority.

gachupines Native Spaniards.

garrison A fort occupied by troops.

Manifest Destiny Movement westward by Anglo settlers to occupy the entire North American continent.

militia A body of citizens enrolled for military service who serve only in emergencies.

missionaries Catholic priests who tried to convert the Native Americans to Christianity.

presidio A Spanish fort that guarded the frontier.

ranchos Ranches or large estates in Mexico.

Tejanos Mexicans living in Texas.

Texians White Texans living in Texas when it was part of Mexico.

FURTHER INFORMATION

BOOKS

Mills, Bronwyn. *U.S.-Mexican War*. New York: Facts on File, 2003.

Teitelbaum, Michael. *Voices from Colonial America, Texas, 1527-1836*.
    Washington: National Geographic, 2005.

Worth, Richard. *Mexican Immigrants*. New York: Facts on File, 2004.

WEB SITES

Handbook of Texas Online
www.tsha.utexas.edu/handbook/online/
Gutiérrez de Lara: Mexican-Texan, The Story of a Creole Hero
www.tamu.edu/ccbn/dewitt/delara.htm
Nueva España
www.tamu.edu/ccbn/dewitt/Spain2.htm
The Virtual Museum of the City of San Francisco
www.sfmuseum.org/

BIBLIOGRAPHY

Brands, H.W. *Lone Star Nation*. New York: Doubleday, 2004.

Campbell, Randolph. *Gone to Texas: A History of the Lone Star State*. New York: Oxford University Press, 2003.

Davis, William. *Lone Star Rising*. New York: Free Press, 2004.

Kessell, John. *Spain in the Southwest*. Norman, OK: University of Oklahoma Press, 2002.

Index

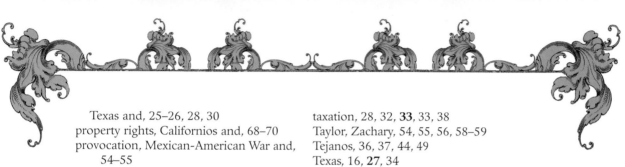

Texas and, 25–26, 28, 30
property rights, Californios and, 68–70
provocation, Mexican-American War and, 54–55
Pueblo Indians, 8

railroads, 72
Republican Army of the North, 17–18, 20
Resaca de la Palma, Battle of, 56
Rio Grande River, 52, 54, 65
Rio San Gabriel, Battle of, 64
Roman Catholic Church, 5, 8, 26, 31
runaway slaves, 33

Salcedo, Manuel María de, 17, 18, 20
Salcedo, Nemesio, 6, 8, 11
San Antonio, **18**, 20, 39, 40–42, 51
San Jacinto, Battle of, 45–47
Santa Anna, Antonio López de, 28, 30, **34**, **46**, 72
    Mexican-American War and, 58, 59, 65
    Spanish invasion of Mexico and, 31
    Texas independence movement and, 35–36, 38
    Texas War for Independence and, 42, 44–45, 45–47
Santa Fe, 5, 10–11, 59, **60**, 61
Santa Fe Trail, 51
Scott, Winfield, 63, 65, **66**
Seguín, Juan, 37, **37**, 44–45, 49
settlers. *See* Anglo settlers; Spanish settlers
Shaler, William, 19, 20
slavery, 27, 30, 32, 33, 51, 52
Slidell, John, 52, 54
soldiers, in Spanish territories, 13–14, 34
Spain, 14, 31
Spanish settlers, 7–8, **9**, 10–11, 61
Spanish territories, 5–11, 13–14
    Mexican independence and, 14, 16, 21, 23
    Texas revolution and, 17–18, 19, 20–21
    See also Mexico
stamps, **72**
statehood, Texas and, 51, 52
Stockton, Robert, 64
Sutter's Fort, 61, 67

taxation, 28, 32, **33**, 33, 38
Taylor, Zachary, 54, 55, 56, 58–59
Tejanos, 36, 37, 44, 49
Texas, 16, **27**, 34
    Anglo settlers and, **24**, 25–26, 30, 32–33
    independence movement and, 35–36, 38
    Louisiana Purchase and, 6
    Mexico and, 26–28, 30
    revolution in, 17–18, 19, 20–21
    War for Independence and, 38–42, 44–47
trade, 9, 10, 27–28, 32, 51
Travis, William, 32–33, 36, **36**, 38, 42, **42–43**, 44
Treaty of Guadalupe Hidalgo, 65, 68
Trist, Nicholas, 65

United States
    Adams-Onis Treaty, 21
    California and, 68–70
    Lone Star Republic and, 51, 52
    Mexican-American War, 52–65
    New Mexico and, 70, 72
    revolution in Texas and, 17–18, 19
    Spanish territories and, 11, 13
Urrea, José de, 45

Veracruz, Mexican-American War and, 63, 65
Verdugo, José Maria, 13–14
Vial, Pedro, 9

Washington-on-the-Brazos, 44

Zambrano, Manuel, 17

ABOUT THE AUTHOR

RICHARD WORTH is the author of more than fifty books, including biographies, historical works, and current events. He has written two books for Marshall Cavendish, *The Arab-Israeli Conflict* and *Workers' Rights*. He is also the author of a biography of Dolores Huerta, the co-founder of the United Farm Workers of America, and a history of Mexican immigration.